A Child's
TRUE STORY OF JESUS

BOOK 1

"COMPILED BY A DOMINICAN SISTER"

EDITED BY
LISA BERGMAN

WITH ADDITIONAL TEXT BY
MOTHER MARY LOYOLA
REV. ALOYSIUS J. HEEG, S.J.

AND NEW ILLUSTRATIONS BY
SAM ESTRADA

2018

ST. AUGUSTINE ACADEMY PRESS
HOMER GLEN, ILLINOIS

Nihil Obstat:

William H. Agnew, S.J.

Censor Deputatus

Imprimatur:

George Cardinal Mundelein

Archbishop of Chicago

May 11, 1928

Dedication

To all the children into whose hands this little
book may fall, with the hope that it may help each
one of them towards the love of Him who said:
"Of Such Is The Kingdom of Heaven."

ISBN: 978-1-64051-066-1

This book was originally published in 1928 by Lawdale Publishing House.
This new revised edition ©2018 by St. Augustine Academy Press.
Illustrations ©2018 by Sam Estrada.

This newly edited edition of *A Child's True Story of Jesus* has been altered slightly from its original format. Besides the addition of decorative features, the following elements were modified:

1. The original illustrations have been retained in most instances, but have been converted to black and white line drawings to allow for coloring by the student.

2. Only captions and paste-in illustrations were included in the original book. Text was therefore added from Book Two and supplemented with the help of passages from the books *My Gift to Jesus* by the same author and *Jesus and I* by Rev. Aloysius J. Heeg, S.J.

3. The Glorious Mysteries were added, along with accompanying text and illustrations.

4. There is no record of any teacher's manual or other instruction being provided with the original book; research in contemporary education journals and analysis of the structure of Book Two in this series were referred to in order to rebuild as closely as possible the intended method.

5. The order of the lessons in the original book (which has been largely retained, except for the additions noted in #3) followed a pattern that suggested itself to the learning of prayers and the Mysteries of the Rosary. Building upon this apparent intent, the prayer cut-out activities were added in order to reinforce the usefulness of the lessons toward this end.

6. Wherever possible, prayers are presented in their traditional wording. However, some, like the Acts of Faith, Hope and Love, the Prayer before a Crucifix and the Spiritual Communion prayer, have been modified to make them more accessible to young children while still embodying the same sentiments. Most of these paraphrases were taken from Mother Mary Loyola's *Little Children's Prayer Book*; the Prayer Before a Crucifix was composed by the editor based on the original prayer.

To the Little One Who Uses This Book:

Chicago, Illinois
June 4, 1928

My dear little Child:

This is your own little book. You have a beautiful picture for each one of your stories. Each one will tell you something about our dear Lord. Remember, Jesus was once a little Child just your age. He was always very kind. He helped His good father. He helped Our Blessed Lady, too. When Jesus grew older, He had very hard work to do for His Father in heaven. Jesus loved you and me so much that He lived for us and He died for us. Now He is waiting for us in Heaven. If we do what pleases Jesus we will be with Him some day.

As I write this little letter I am praying that our dear Lord may bless you. He will bless you because He loves you. Ask Jesus to bless the whole world.

Your friend,

Daniel F. Cunningham

Rev. Daniel F. Cunningham
Superintendent of Schools

FOR TEACHERS AND PARENTS

A *Child's True Story of Jesus* was first published in two volumes in 1928. Using a method of instruction called *Arbeitsprinzip*, which means "learning by doing," the author, Sister Mary Ambrose, sought to provide a way of introducing an active principle into the study of religion for young children. In both books, she used variations of a "Story Picture Method," in which the instructor reads a story to the child to first engage the attention and imagination. Then a picture illustrating the story is shown, and the child is invited to use the picture to help retell the story in his or her own words. Lastly, the child would paste the picture into the book, following pre-printed "legends" at the bottom of each page.

We were fortunate to obtain an unused copy of the second volume in the series, and were able to deduce something of the intended method from all the pieces, though no teacher's manual or other instructions were provided. Research in contemporary education journals also gave us many helpful clues.

However, this first volume contained only pictures and a "legend," or caption, for each picture at the bottom of each page. No story was provided, so the paste-in text that was provided for Book Two has been borrowed, and where it was deemed too sparse, we supplemented it, based on portions of text from another book by the same author (*My Gift to Jesus*), as well as the book *Jesus and I* by Rev. Aloysius Heeg, S.J..

The color illustrations in both volumes were lovely choices, but suffered from very poor print quality, and thus were limited in their usefulness. It therefore made sense to convert these into line drawings, as the opportunity to color them added an additional activity for the child.

However, while we kept these pictures at their original size in Book Two, so that they could be cut out and pasted in their places, in Book One it seemed best to expand these illustrations to the size of a full page in order to make them easier for young children to color. Of course, at this size, cutting them out and pasting them became impractical. Nevertheless, we wanted Book One to be more than merely a coloring book.

As we further analyzed the structure of the book, it became apparent that the order of the lessons seemed to lend itself to the teaching of basic prayers as well as the Mysteries of the Rosary. Based on this clear outline, we reintroduced the cutting and pasting activity as a way of reinforcing the memorization of the prayers and Mysteries. We added in the Glorious Mysteries (which were not present in the original Book One) and sought additional opportunities within the book to teach other age-appropriate prayers, especially during the Mass.

So although these prayer pages were not found in the original Book One, we do earnestly believe that they are entirely in keeping with the intentions of the original author, both in terms of content and activity. Both Book One and Book Two work well with each other, yet at the same time, each has its own different focus for its own age group.

While we typically are very careful never to modify the works we republish, we hope all will agree that this was unavoidable under the circumstances, and we pray that in our attempt to reconstruct this activity book, we have truly added value to the original material. Until and unless the original instructions should be discovered, we feel this is a reasonable compromise.

In Christ,
Lisa Bergman
St. Augustine Academy Press
December 2018

HOW TO USE THIS BOOK

There are three types of pages in this book. Some pages teach a Lesson and others teach Prayers or the Mysteries of the Rosary.

Jesus Prayed.
Jesus helped His friends to pray.
Jesus told his friends to ask God
  to help them.
Jesus taught us what to say.
He said:

Our Father Who art in heaven;
  hallowed be Thy name;
Thy kingdom come;
Thy will be done
  on earth as it is in heaven.
Give us this day our daily bread;
And forgive us our trespasses,
  as we forgive those
  who trespass against us;
And lead us not into temptation
But deliver us from evil. Amen.

"Our Father Who Art in Heaven"

1. LESSON PAGES

Read the lesson aloud with the help of a teacher, parent or other friend.
Then look at the illustration and retell the story in your own words,
using the picture to help you! Enjoy coloring the picture.

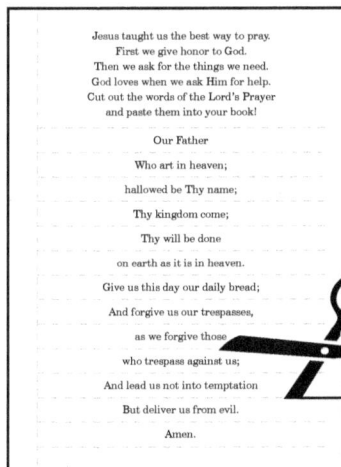

Jesus taught us the best way to pray.
First we give honor to God.
Then we ask for the things we need.
God loves when we ask Him for help.
Cut out the words of the Lord's Prayer
and paste them into your book!

Our Father

Who art in heaven;

hallowed be Thy name;

Thy kingdom come;

Thy will be done

on earth as it is in heaven.

Give us this day our daily bread;

And forgive us our trespasses,

as we forgive those

who trespass against us;

And lead us not into temptation

But deliver us from evil.

Amen.

THE LORD'S PRAYER

2. CUTOUT PAGES → 3. PRAYER PAGES

Here you will find prayers to learn and lists of the Mysteries of the Rosary. Work on memorizing them one or two lines at a time. Cut out the words along the dotted lines.

Arrange the words of each prayer in order on the Prayer Pages. For the Mysteries of the Rosary, arrange them in order and match them up with their descriptions. Paste these in your book.

Jesus Prayed.

Jesus helped His friends to pray.

Jesus told his friends to ask God
    to help them.

Jesus taught us what to say.

He said:

Our Father Who art in heaven;
    hallowed be Thy name;

Thy kingdom come;

Thy will be done
    on earth as it is in heaven.

Give us this day our daily bread;

And forgive us our trespasses,
    as we forgive those
    who trespass against us;

And lead us not into temptation

But deliver us from evil. Amen.

"Our Father Who Art in Heaven"

Jesus taught us the best way to pray.
First we give honor to God.
Then we ask for the things we need.
God loves when we ask Him for help.
Cut out the words of the Lord's Prayer
and paste them into your book!

Our Father

Who art in heaven;

hallowed be Thy name;

Thy kingdom come;

Thy will be done

on earth as it is in heaven.

Give us this day our daily bread;

And forgive us our trespasses,

as we forgive those

who trespass against us;

And lead us not into temptation

But deliver us from evil.

Amen.

THE LORD'S PRAYER

Mary was praying.

She was asking God to help her.

God sent an angel to Mary.

The angel told Mary that God would
   send her a little Son.

This is why we say the "Hail Mary."

The angel said:
   "Hail Mary, full of grace!
   the Lord is with thee."

"Hail Mary, Full of Grace."

Mary went to visit her cousin,
    Elizabeth.
Elizabeth was happy to see Mary.
She greeted Mary by saying,
    "Blessed art thou amongst women,
    and blessed is the fruit of thy womb."

Jesus wants us to ask Mary to help us.
We say:
    "Holy Mary, Mother of God,
    pray for us sinners,
    now and at the hour of our death.
    Amen."

The Mother of Jesus Visits Her
Cousin, St. Elizabeth.

The Angel's words to Mary are the start of this prayer.
Its proper name is the *Angelic Salutation*.
We call it the "Hail Mary."
Cut out the words of the Hail Mary
and paste them into your book!

Hail Mary

Full of Grace

The Lord is with Thee;

Blessed art Thou among Women,

And Blessed is the

Fruit of Thy Womb, Jesus.

Holy Mary

Mother of God

Pray for us sinners,

Now and at the hour of our death.

Amen.

THE ANGELIC SALUTATION
HAIL MARY

Joseph and Mary had to go far away
from home.

They went to Bethlehem.

Joseph was kind to Mary.

He wanted to find her a place to rest
for the night.

The people in the houses said,
"There is no room."

So Mary and Joseph had to go into a
poor stable.

In that poor stable Jesus was born.

This was the first Christmas.

God loved Mary and Joseph.

Jesus made them happy.

The Baby Jesus is Born in a
Stable at Bethlehem.

The Shepherds were kind men.

They watched the sheep.

God loved these good men.

Bright angels came from heaven.

They told the shepherds the wonderful

    story of the new little Savior.

They told the shepherds where to find

    Jesus, lying in a manger.

The angels sang:

    "Glory to God in the highest

    and peace on earth to men."

Beautiful Angels Come from Heaven.
Now the Shepherds Know the Wonderful Story.

A song like the one the Angels sang,
which gives glory to God in Three Persons,
is called a *Doxology*.
We often pray a doxology. It is called the "Glory Be."
Cut out the words of the "Glory Be"
and paste them into your book!

Glory be to the Father,

And to the Son,

And to the Holy Spirit,

As it was in the beginning,

Is now,

And ever shall be,

World without end.

Amen.

THE DOXOLOGY
GLORY BE

Joseph and Mary bring Jesus to the
Temple.

They present Him to God.

They offer a sacrifice for him.

They offer two turtledoves.

Old Simeon sees Baby Jesus and knows
he is God's Son.

He is glad to see Him.

He gives thanks to God for His Gift to
the world.

Mary Brings Jesus to the Priest
in the Temple.

Joseph and Mary obey the law.

They went to the Temple to pray.

Jesus went with Mary and Joseph.

Jesus is happy to be with Mary and
   Joseph.

This makes Mary and Joseph happy, too.

The Temple was a large building.

Jesus stayed in the Temple.

Mary could not find Jesus.

Joseph could not find Jesus.

Soon Jesus saw his father and Mother
   coming for him.

Jesus was talking about God.

Jesus obeyed Joseph and Mary.

Jesus went home with Mary and
   Joseph.

Jesus Talks to the Teachers in the
Temple. He Asks Them Questions.

THE JOYFUL MYSTERIES
OF THE ROSARY

The first Joyful Mystery is

This is when

The second Joyful Mystery is

This is when

The five wonderful events that we just learned about
make up the five Joyful Mysteries of the Rosary.
Cut out the names of the Mysteries, match them with
their descriptions, and paste them into your book!

The Annunciation

The Visitation

The Nativity

The Presentation in the Temple

The Finding of the Child Jesus in the Temple

The Angel announces to Mary that

she will bear baby Jesus.

Mary goes to visit her cousin Elizabeth.

Jesus is born in Bethlehem.

Mary and Joseph present Jesus

to the priest in the Temple.

Mary and Joseph find Jesus talking

to the teachers in the Temple.

The third Joyful Mystery is

This is when

The fourth Joyful Mystery is

This is when

The fifth Joyful Mystery is

This is when

Mary was resting.

Jesus was resting, too.

An angel wakens Joseph and tells him
to take Mary and Jesus away.

Joseph obeyed.

Mary obeyed, too.

Joseph took Mary and Jesus into
Egypt.

God asks me to obey, too.

Jesus, Mary and Joseph,
help me to be good and obey
like you.

An Angel Told Joseph to Go with
Mary and Jesus into Egypt.

King Herod sent his soldiers to
  Bethlehem.
He was jealous of Jesus.
But the Angel made Jesus safe from
  King Herod.
He showed Joseph the way to Egypt.

Mary prayed on the way to Egypt.
She was so good, she even prayed for
  King Herod.

Mary wants us always to be good.
She will help us, if we pray to her.
She is glad to hear us say:
  "Pray for us sinners."

An Angel Shows Joseph
the Way to Egypt.

An angel came to Mary.

Angels took care of Joseph and Mary.

An angel told the shepherds the
wonderful story.

God sent an angel to help Joseph.

Joseph saved Jesus.

God sends an angel from heaven to
help me, too.

He is called my Guardian Angel.

My good angel wants to help me be
good.

I will pray to my Guardian Angel.

I will ask him to help me.

My Guardian Angel

Our Good Angel is always watching over us.
We should pray to him and ask for his help.
Cut out the words of the Guardian Angel prayer
and paste them into your book!

Angel of God,

My Guardian Dear,

To Whom God's Love

Commits me here;

Ever this day

Be at my side,

To Light,

To Guard,

To Rule and Guide.

Amen.

PRAYER TO
MY GUARDIAN ANGEL

Jesus helped his Mother.

Mary kept the little home of Nazareth
very clean.

Jesus helped His Mother with her work.

When the work was done, Jesus talked
to Mary.

Jesus was happy at home.

He made his father and Mother happy,
too.

Jesus became a child so that I could
learn from him.

I will help my Mother, too.

Help me, Jesus, to be like you.

Jesus is Helping Mary.

Jesus is working.

He is helping His father.

The home of Joseph was a work shop.

Mary watched Jesus at His work.

Jesus carried the wood for Joseph.

Joseph was an old man.

Jesus was kind to him.

I can help my father with little jobs,
    too.

Help me, Jesus, to be like you.

Jesus is Helping Joseph.

Jesus, Mary and Joseph loved to pray.

They prayed every morning.

They prayed every night.

They said little prayers all through the day.

Jesus loved to talk to His Father in
Heaven by praying.

Jesus showed us how to be good.

He prayed well. He worked well.
He played well.

Jesus wants us to do as he did.

He wants us to pray well, to work well,
to play well.

We can do everything well if we do
everything for Jesus.

We can say "All for Thee, O Jesus."

Mary loves to see us do this.

She hurries to help us when we pray
the Hail Mary.

Jesus is Praying.
This Makes Mary Happy.

Jesus became a little child to set a good example for us.
We can be like Him by offering all that we do to God.
Cut out the words of the Morning Offering prayer
and paste them into your book!

My God, I offer Thee this day

All I shall think, or do, or say,

Uniting it with what was done

On Earth by Jesus Christ Thy Son.

MY MORNING OFFERING

Children love Jesus and like to be
near him.

Once the Apostles wanted them to go
away because Jesus was tired.

But he loved the children and was
never too tired for them.

He said, "Let the little ones come
to Me."

How lucky were the little children who
could sit on Jesus' lap!

But we can come to Jesus, too.

We can see the little door to His House
on the altar in church.

He lives there so that He can be close
to us always.

I will visit Him there. He will be happy
when I come to see Him.

"Let the Little Ones Come to Me."

Jesus saw that the woman was sad.

Her only son was dead.

He felt pity for her.

He made her son well again.

The people were filled with joy and
awe.

They praised God.

Jesus always loved to help people.

He wanted to show them what God
could do for them if they love him
and trust in Him.

I will offer God my Acts of Faith, Hope
and Love.

I will try always to love and trust in
Him.

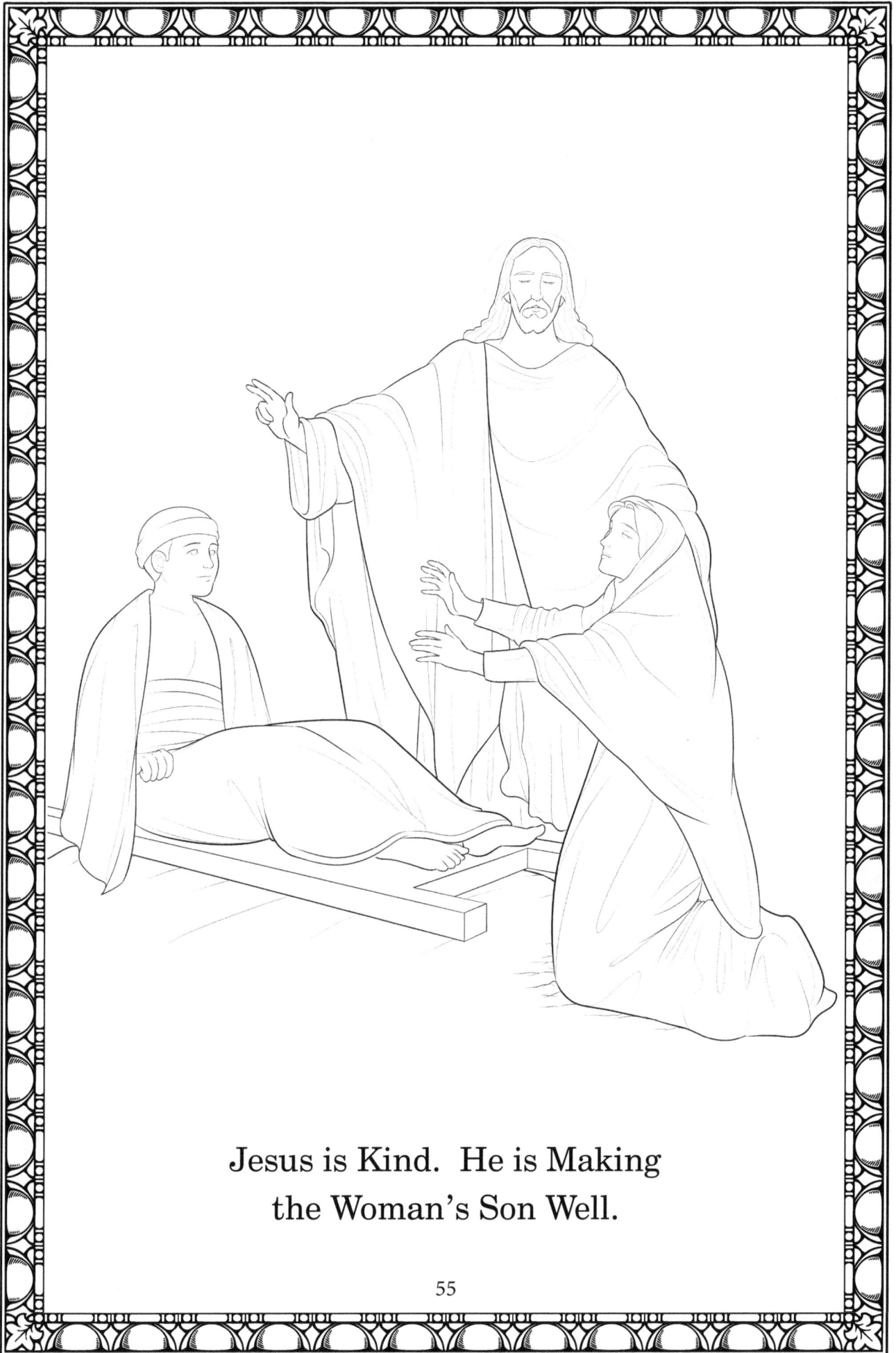

Jesus is Kind. He is Making
the Woman's Son Well.

When we visit Jesus in Church, we can tell Him that we love and trust him with special prayers.
Cut out the words of the Acts of Faith, Hope and Love and paste them into your book!

My God, I believe in Thee,

because Thou art Truth itself.

My God, I hope in Thee,

because of Thy promises to me.

My God, I love Thee,

because Thou art so good.

Teach me to love Thee daily more and more,

And to love everybody for Thy sake.

MY ACT OF FAITH

MY ACT OF HOPE

MY ACT OF LOVE

The friends of Jesus sleep.

They forget to pray.

Jesus is sad.

He is praying for me.

He is alone.

God sends an angel from Heaven to
    comfort Jesus.

We can help all who suffer by our
    prayers.

Let us remember our dear ones.

Let us not forget those who are
    suffering in Purgatory.

We can help them by our prayers.

Jesus is Sad. He is
Praying for Us.

When Jesus was lonely and sad, His friends forgot to pray.
We must not forget to pray for our loved ones.
Cut out the words of the Prayer for the Souls in
Purgatory and paste them into your book!

Eternal rest grant unto them, O Lord,

And let perpetual light shine upon them.

May their souls,

And the souls of all the faithful departed,

Rest in Peace. Amen.

PRAYER FOR THE SOULS
IN PURGATORY

Jesus was brought before Pilate.

He wanted to let Jesus go.

But the crowds shouted "Crucify Him!"

So Pilate had his soldiers punish Jesus.

They used whips to hurt him.

Jesus was punished for my sins.

I am sorry, Jesus.

Help me always to be good.

Help me never to hurt you.

Wicked Men Punish Jesus.

The soldiers were done whipping Jesus.

They made a crown out of thorns.

They put it on Jesus.

Then they laughed at Him and were
     mean to Him.

Jesus did not try to stop them.

Sometimes I am mean to others.

Help me to think of you instead, Jesus.

Help me never to hurt you.

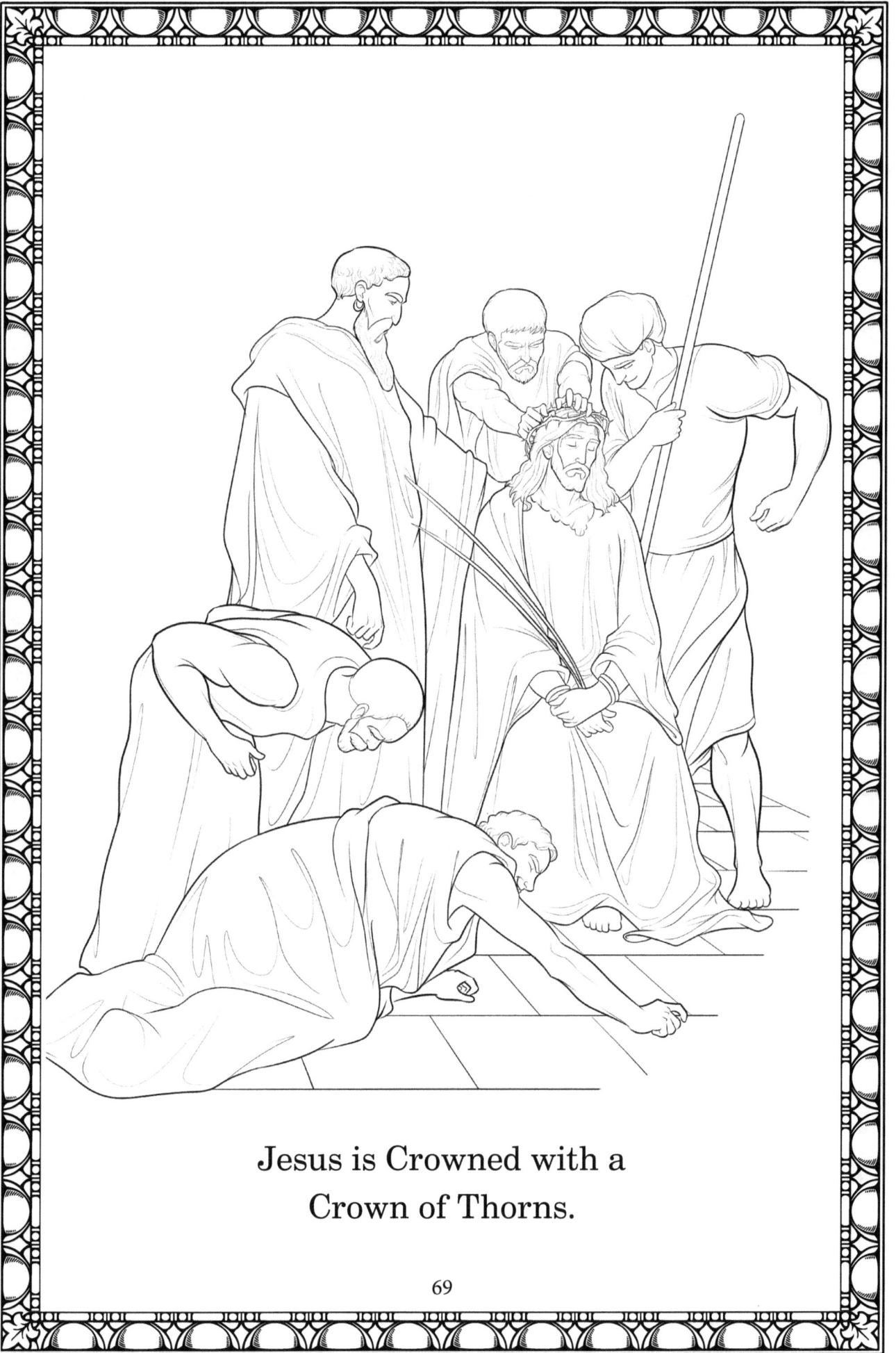

Jesus is Crowned with a
Crown of Thorns.

The soldiers made Jesus carry his cross.

It was very heavy.

He fell three times.

He saw his Mother.

She was sad.

The women of Jerusalem were sad, too.

Poor Jesus!

His cross was heavy because of our sins.

Help me to be good, Jesus.

Help me never to hurt you.

Jesus Carries His Cross.

The soldiers nailed Jesus to the Cross.

He forgave them.

He stayed on the cross for three hours.

All that pain, for me!

He looked up to God in Heaven.

He said:

"Into Thy Hands

I commend My Spirit."

Then Jesus died.

Jesus Loves Us.

He Died on the Cross for Us.

THE SORROWFUL MYSTERIES
OF THE ROSARY

The first Sorrowful Mystery is

This is when

The second Sorrowful Mystery is

This is when

The five sad events that we just learned about make up
the five Sorrowful Mysteries of the Rosary.
Cut out the names of the Mysteries, match them with
their descriptions, and paste them into your book!

The Agony in the Garden

The Scourging at the Pillar

The Crowning with Thorns

The Carrying of the Cross

The Crucifixion

Jesus is Sad.

He is Praying for us.

Wicked Men Punish Jesus.

Jesus is crowned

with a Crown of Thorns.

Jesus Carries His Cross.

Jesus Died on the Cross for Us.

The third Sorrowful Mystery is

This is when

The fourth Sorrowful Mystery is

This is when

The fifth Sorrowful Mystery is

This is when

Three days after Jesus was buried,

    He rose from His grave.

Some holy women went to visit His grave,

    but when they got there, an angel said,

    "He is not here,

      for He is risen, as He said."

Jesus is God.

He promises that one day I will rise

    from the grave, too.

I want to be with Jesus in heaven.

I know Jesus will keep his promises.

I say, "O Jesus, I hope in Thee."

He Is Risen.

God sent Jesus to be with us on earth.

When Jesus' work was done on earth,

He went to God in Heaven.

His Apostles do His work here.

Heaven is that beautiful home where

Jesus now lives.

He loves us so much that He wants us

to live there too.

He wants us to live there forever.

But Jesus can not take us into heaven

unless we are good.

Can we all be good?

Yes, because Jesus promised to help us.

That is why we say:

"O Jesus, I hope in Thee."

Jesus Goes to Heaven.

Jesus promised his disciples he would
  not leave them all alone.
When He went back to heaven, He
  promised to send them the Holy Ghost
  to comfort them and teach them.
Jesus begins the Church by sending
  the Holy Ghost to help the Apostles.

Kings send messengers with great
  power.
Jesus sends the Holy Ghost with all the
  power of Heaven.

I believe what Jesus tells me through
  His Church.
I say, "O Jesus, I believe in Thee."

Jesus Sends the Holy Ghost
to Help the Apostles.

Jesus was kind to Mary when He was a
little Boy.
Jesus was sorry when His Mother was
sad.

Mary was lonely without Jesus.
Jesus sends angels to bring His Mother
to Heaven.

Jesus loves me and wants me to be in
Heaven with Him too.
He will help me to be good if I ask Him.
He comes to us at Mass.
I will go to Mass.
I will tell Him,
"O Jesus, I love Thee with all my
heart."

Jesus Takes His Mother
to Heaven.

85

God chose Mary to be the Mother of
His Son, Jesus.

Mary was the most beautiful woman
that was ever known.

When Jesus suffered for us, Mary
suffered too.

Now Jesus is King of Heaven and
earth.

Jesus left his Mother to us.

He makes her His Queen and our
Queen in Heaven.

Jesus Makes Mary Queen
of Heaven.

THE GLORIOUS MYSTERIES
OF THE ROSARY

The first Glorious Mystery is

This is when

The second Glorious Mystery is

This is when

The five amazing events that we just learned about
make up the five Glorious Mysteries of the Rosary.
Cut out the names of the Mysteries, match them with
their descriptions, and paste them into your book!

The Resurrection

The Ascension

The Descent of the Holy Spirit

The Assumption

The Coronation

Jesus is Risen.

Jesus Goes to Heaven.

Jesus Sends the Holy Ghost

to Help the Apostles.

Jesus Takes His Mother

to Heaven.

Jesus Makes Mary Queen

of Heaven.

The third Glorious Mystery is

This is when

The fourth Glorious Mystery is

This is when

The fifth Glorious Mystery is

This is when

I go to Mass.

Jesus will be there.

I must be ready to meet Him.

I must be good.

I must be polite.

It is polite to be on time.

I will be polite at Mass.

I will arrive early to prepare my heart

for Jesus.

It is Polite to Be on Time.

93

I come to Church.

Jesus is present here.

He lives in His little home on the Altar.

I will think of this when I enter the
Church.

I bless myself with holy water.

I genuflect and tell Him,

"I adore You, my Jesus on the altar.
You are the Son of God and the Son
of the Virgin Mary."

"I Adore You, My Jesus
on the Altar."

I come to Church.

I see the crucifix.

It reminds me that Jesus died for me so
that I could go to heaven.

Jesus, hanging on the cross for me,
I love You!

I am sorry for having offended You.

I will think of You at Mass.

Jesus is Hanging on the Cross.

Whenever we see a Crucifix we should thank Jesus
for his sacrifice for us with this special prayer.
Cut out the words of the Prayer before a Crucifix
and paste them into your book!

Dear Jesus, look down on me, your little child.

I kneel before You, sad and sorry.

You died on the cross to take away my sins.

Help me never to hurt you again through sin.

I kiss the wounds in your hands.

I kiss the wounds in your feet.

I kiss the wound in your side.

Please help me to love, trust and obey God

As You did. Amen.

PRAYER BEFORE A CRUCIFIX

On the cross, Jesus offered the
Sacrifice to God.

He asks me to come to Mass.

At Mass the priest offers Jesus's
Sacrifice to God.

I must pray to God at Mass.

I honor God.

I thank God.

I ask him to bless me.

Jesus Prayed to God.
I Must Pray to God at Mass.

The priest is going to offer Jesus'
    sacrifice to God.

He wants to be ready to hold Jesus' body
    in his hands.

He wants his soul to be spotless.

He is asking God to pardon his sins.

I must ask God to pardon my sins.

I will say an Act of Contrition.

The Priest is Asking God
to Pardon His Sins.

Jesus promised to forgive our sins if we are truly sorry.
This prayer is a good way of telling Him so.
Cut out the words of the Act of Contrition
and paste them into your book!

O my God,

I am heartily sorry

for having offended Thee.

I detest all my sins

because I dread the loss of heaven

and the pains of hell.

But most of all because

they offend Thee, my God,

Who art all good and

deserving of all my love.

I firmly resolve,

with the help of Thy grace

to sin no more, and to avoid

the near occasions of sin. Amen.

ACT OF CONTRITION

The priest is reading the letters of the
    Apostles.
I will listen.

St. Paul writes: "Children, obey your
    parents in the Lord for this is right."
Jesus is my example.
He was obedient to His Heavenly
    Father.
He obeyed Mary and Joseph.
I shall obey.
Jesus, Mary and Joseph, teach me to be
    obedient.

The Priest is Reading the Letters
of the Apostles.

The Gospel is the word of God.

The priest will read God's words to His
   people.

I rise when the priest reads the Gospel.

I promise to:

   keep the Word of God in my mind,

   defend it in my speech,

   and love it in my heart.

I will often talk about God.

I will love to hear about Him.

The Priest is Reading the
Word of God.

The most important part of the Mass is
now beginning.

I will keep my eyes on the altar.

The priest is offering God bread.

God will change the bread into the
Body of Jesus.

The priest is offering this bread for
himself and for all who are in the
Church.

I will make my offering to God, too.

I offer my heart to You, Jesus.

Help me to be good.

The Priest is Offering
Bread to God.

The priest mixes wine and water.

This reminds us that Jesus became
man for us.

The wine represents the part of Jesus
that is God.

The water represents the part of Jesus
that is human.

God will change the wine into the
Blood of Jesus.

He gave His Precious Blood for me.

I will put my special prayers into the
wine along with the drops of water.

Then the priest can offer them to God
along with the wine.

The Priest Takes
Wine and Water.

The priest is offering God wine.

He is offering all our prayers too.

Soon the bread and wine will be the

Body and Blood of Jesus.

I say with the priest:

"Come, Holy Ghost!

Bless this sacrifice which we offer

for the glory of God."

The Priest is Offering
Wine to God.

The priest is washing his hands.

Before I receive Jesus in Holy
    Communion,
I must wash my sins away by
    Confession.

Dear Jesus, You have said:
    "Blessed are the clean of heart,
    for they shall see God."
Make my heart pure.
Make me think of what is right.
Keep me close to You.
May I never displease You again.

The Priest is Washing
His Hands.

The priest is looking up.

He is holding the Body of Jesus.

Jesus gave His Life for me.

The servers ring the bell.

I will look up and say:

"My Lord and my God."

I adore Thee, O sacred Body of Jesus.

You are my Lord and My God.

I believe in Thee, I hope in Thee,

I love Thee with all my heart.

"My Lord and My God!"

The priest lifts the Chalice.

It holds the Blood of Jesus.

I believe this.

Poor Jesus!

He shed His Precious Blood for me.

The servers ring the bell again.

I will look up and say:

"My Jesus, Mercy!"

I adore Thee, O Sacred Blood of Jesus.

You are the price of my salvation.

Keep my soul free from sin.

"My Jesus, Mercy!"

The priest is receiving Jesus.

I wish I were receiving Him, too.

Take my heart, dear Jesus.

Keep me from hurting you.

I bow my head and say:

"Dearest Jesus, meek and mild,

O come to me, Your little child!

Make me pure and good like Thee,

Come, my Jesus, come to me!"

The Priest is Receiving Jesus.

The priest is showing Jesus to me.

Bless me, Jesus.

May Your Body and Blood keep me

from doing what is wrong.

I say with the priest,

"Lord, I am not worthy that

Thou shouldst come under my roof;

But only say the word,

And my soul shall be healed."

Jesus is Blessing Me.

The children are receiving Jesus.

I am going to receive Him someday too.

Now I will invite Him to come into my
heart.

He will be happy.

He will make me happy, too.

I will tell Him what I need.

The Children Are Receiving Jesus.

Jesus comes to us in the Holy Eucharist.
Even if you cannot receive Communion,
He can come into your heart if you invite Him.
Cut out the words of the Spiritual Communion Prayer
and paste them into your book!

I believe, dear Jesus,

that You are really present

in the most holy Sacrament.

I adore Thee.

I love Thee.

I desire to receive Thee.

Come into my heart

and never leave me.

Come, Lord Jesus, come!

I give you my heart and my soul.

SPIRITUAL COMMUNION PRAYER

You always loved to be with little
   children, dear Jesus.
Please come to me and stay with me.
Please help me to be good.

I will spend some time with Jesus now.
I will be like the little children who
   climbed on Jesus' lap.

I will tell Him that I love Him.
I will tell Him what I need.

Jesus Loves to Be with Little Children.

The priest is giving me God's blessing.

I will ask God to bless my dear ones.

I will make the Sign of the Cross.

In the name of the Father, and of the
Son, and of the Holy Ghost. Amen.

The Priest is Giving Me
God's Blessing.

The priest is telling me, Jesus is God.

I believe this.

If I receive Jesus often, I will be a child
    of God.

I thank God.

Dear Jesus, I am going away.

I will think of You often.

I am sorry You suffered so much.

I will be back to visit You again soon.

Help me to think of You often.

Listen to the Word of God.

Jesus wants me to be a good child
always.

He wants me to obey my father and
mother.

He obeyed His father and mother on
Earth and in Heaven.

I will obey, Jesus.

Help me to be good.

I Will Obey.

THE TEN
COMMANDMENTS

I

II

III

IV

V

God gave us Ten Commandments
so that we would know how to obey Him.
Cut out each of the Ten Commandments
and paste them into your book!

1. I am the Lord your God; you shall not have

   strange gods before Me.

2. You shall not take the Name of the Lord

   your God in vain.

3. Remember to keep holy the Lord's day.

4. Honor your father and your mother.

5. You shall not kill.

6. You shall not commit adultery.

7. You shall not steal.

8. You shall not bear false witness against

   your neighbour.

9. You shall not covet your neighbour's wife.

10. You shall not covet your neighbour's goods.

THE TEN COMMANDMENTS

VI

VII

VIII

IX

X

www.ingramcontent.com/pod-product-compliance
Lightning Source LLC
LaVergne TN
LVHW081316060426
835509LV00015B/1547